AMAZING TRUE DOG STORIES

LOUIS SABIN

SCHOLASTIC INC.
New York Toronto London Auckland Sydney Tokyo

Just for Fran

ISBN 0-590-31542-0

Copyright © 1983 by Louis Sabin.
All rights reserved. Published by Scholastic Inc.

12 11 10 9 8 7 6 5 4 3 2 1   11   3 4 5 6 7/8

Contents

1

Bubblegum and the Ducks

Dogs often make friends with other four-legged animals. But it's not too often that a puppy takes to *ducks* — so much so that he tries to be one!

Ken Matthews and his sister Lori, of Topeka, Kansas, were on a family camping trip when they heard a whining sound.

"It's coming from behind that big rock," Ken said, pointing. "Let's see what it is."

What they found behind the rock, huddled on a pile of rags, was a tiny brown puppy. While Lori stroked the puppy's head, Ken ran to tell his parents. They came back with him, and his mother exclaimed, "Why, this pup is only a few days old! Either the mother has deserted it, or she's had an accident. If she isn't back by the time we have to leave, we'll take the puppy with us."

Back home at their farm, Ken and Lori filled a large cardboard box with torn-up newspapers for the puppy's bed, and placed it near the kitchen stove.

Then Lori poured some warm milk into a bowl and offered it to the pup. The little dog lowered his head and sniffed the milk eagerly, but he didn't know how to drink.

"What are we going to do?" asked Ken. "We don't want him to starve."

"Don't worry." Mrs. Matthews laughed. "I still have the baby bottles you and Lori used when you were infants. You can feed him with one of those."

The children took turns holding the bottle while the little pup sucked the milk greedily. Then he curled up in a corner of his box and went to sleep.

Ken and Lori watched him, trying to decide on

a name. Just then the sleeping pup rolled over on his back. Stuck to his stomach was a piece of bubblegum. Lori giggled. "That's what we'll call him," she said. "Bubblegum."

Ken agreed, and the name "stuck."

Three times that evening Bubblegum woke up and whimpered to be fed and petted. And three times the children warmed a baby bottle of milk, fed it to Bubblegum, and stroked his soft fur. But it grew late, and they had to go to bed, too.

"Ar-roooo . . . ar-rooooo," came the wail from the kitchen. "Ar-roooooo . . . yip-yip ar-rooooo" rang through the dark house. All the Matthewses came running, worried about their new "baby." But as soon as they turned on the light, they saw that Bubblegum was fine. He was just wide-awake and wanted company near him.

"This won't do," grumbled Mr. Matthews sleepily. "We need quiet at night. So, Mr. Bubblegum, I'm taking you out of here. The cows and chickens and ducks won't mind your singing." And he carried Bubblegum's box out to the barn.

Ken and Lori expected to hear more howls. But right away the little puppy settled down to living in the barn. He didn't cry or howl at all. When Lori or Ken came to feed him, he ate happily. He slept a lot, and when he was awake he watched the other animals. Most of all, he watched the ducks. And the mother duck watched Bubblegum. She pushed fresh straw into his box. Once she even brought him some of her food. She seemed to know that Bubblegum needed special care.

After school one day, Lori went to the barn to see Bubblegum. She opened the barn door and stared, trying not to laugh.

Across the barn floor came a crooked line of marchers. The mother duck was leading the way. Her head high, she waddled across the wooden floor. Behind her, in an S-shaped line, came her ducklings — four of them, bright yellow and covered with soft down. As the marching ducks passed his box, Bubblegum barked excitedly.

But the parade didn't stop. It waddled by, heading for the other side of the barn. Bubblegum was upset. He wanted to play, too. "Come back," he barked.

The mother duck looked back at Bubblegum. Then she quacked. Bubblegum tried to jump over the side of the box. He didn't make it, but the force of his body tilted the box, and he fell out with a *thump!*

Bubblegum shook his head and stood up, swaying dizzily. Then, his legs wobbly under him, he tried to catch up with the ducks. It took him a few minutes, but he finally made it to the end of the line and became the last "duck" in the parade.

Lori managed not to laugh out loud. Bubble-gum was trying to waddle, too. His feet flopped this way and that. His butterball of a body seemed to roll along, like a bouncing balloon.

Around and around they went — the duck, her ducklings, and Bubblegum. When the mother duck looked back and saw Bubblegum at the end of the line, she showed no surprise; she seemed to expect it.

Lori dashed to the house to get Ken, but the parade was over when they got back. The duck was in her part of the barn, her babies close by. And Bubblegum was stretched out on the floor right next to them. He looked as limp as a wet mop.

Lori and Ken left some dinner for Bubblegum that evening. Afterward they tried to play with him, but he was too tired. He tried to jump up and run to please them, but parade drill had worn him out.

The next day after school, Lori found Bub-blegum with the ducks again. When they moved around the barn, he moved with them. When they settled down, he stayed close by; and the mother duck was treating him like one of her flock. When he got out of line, she quacked at him. She even pecked him when he didn't do what she wanted. And he did his best to obey.

Lori could see that Bubblegum thought he was a duck. He had needed a mother, and the mother duck was happy to oblige. Now she treated him as if he belonged to her.

As the weeks went by, Bubblegum-the-duck tried to fly. He saw his "mother and brothers and sisters" flapping their wings, and he flapped his. Bubblegum's "wings" were his front legs for a while. He stood on his back legs and waved his front legs in the air. It was the closest he could come to doing what the ducks were doing. When this didn't work, he started kicking backwards with his rear legs. But this action still didn't get him off the ground.

He looked so clumsy, trying to fly, that Ken and Lori invited their friends to come and see silly old Bubblegum do his act. They laughed, and Bubblegum barked back. He liked having all this company. But the mother duck didn't. She herded her children further into the barn, and Bubblegum followed them.

Bubblegum's life as a duck kept right on. His quack was still a bark. His walk was nothing like a waddle. His swimming style in the pond was a lot different from the style of his feathered family. He liked his kind of food better than the kind the ducks ate, but this didn't bother him. And it didn't bother his "mother." She seemed quite content that he ate and didn't make any trouble for her.

It looked as if Bubblegum might stay a duck for the rest of his life — until the day the Matthews family had a visit from some cousins. The cousins brought a dog with them. It was their nine-year-old sheep dog.

At first, Bubblegum treated the visitor like a strange sort of animal. But after an hour or so, the sheep dog's smell must have told him something he had not known before. This four-footed animal had the same kind of smell as Bubblegum. And he was fun to run and play with.

When the sheep dog left, Bubblegum went back to being a funny kind of duck. Only things were different now. He tried to get his brothers and sisters to run with him . . . but they couldn't. He tried to get them to roll over and play-fight with him. But they couldn't do that, either. Bubblegum felt confused and unhappy. He missed the sheep dog.

The Matthews family talked about it. "There's only one thing to do," Mr. Matthews decided. "We'll have to get a friend for Bubblegum. A dog friend."

Everyone agreed that this was a fine idea. So that weekend, they bought a little female puppy.

She had spotted paws and big brown eyes. Ken and Lori thought she was beautiful. So did Bubblegum. One look at her and he was in love forever.

Eight years went by. Then in 1977, Lori got married and went to live on a farm several miles away. The day she moved she took a part of home with her — one of Bubblegum's own puppies. But first she had to promise everyone she wouldn't raise it with the ducks on her farm.

2

Champion Rumpelstiltskin: Smart Dog

Most dogs are smart in one way or another. This story is about Champion Rumpelstiltskin, who gave new meaning to the words "smart dog!"

The standard poodle with the fairy-tale name lived with Mrs. Milton S. Erlanger for thirteen years. And in that time he performed some truly amazing acts.

The most mystifying of them all was a mind-reading act, which Rumpelstiltskin performed for the entertainment of Mrs. Erlanger's guests. The dog was told to leave the room and not return until called. Of course, the dog would obey instantly. While he was out, one of the guests would pull a playing card from a 52-card deck. Another guest would tell everyone what the card was (for example, the ten of spades) and then put it back in the deck. After that, all fifty-two cards were spread out on the floor.

As soon as everybody had moved away from the cards, Rumpelstiltskin would be called back into the room. Told to find the "mystery card," the curly-haired dog would bark once as if saying "Yes!" and then would look over the cards. He never took more than a few seconds to make his choice — and he always picked the right card! Was it a trick, or did Rumpelstiltskin have ESP (extrasensory perception)? Some of the guests thought he did.

This wise and wonderful poodle also helped out around the house. Whenever people came to visit, he was right on hand to take their hats and hang them on pegs. Then he would trot back for their gloves. He would carry these gently in his mouth and lay them on top of a table near the front door.

If the guests stayed for dinner, they were in for an additional treat: the sight of Rumpelstiltskin carrying dishes from the dinner table to the kitchen. Rumpelstiltskin never dropped a dish or slopped any leftover food or coffee.

Rumpelstiltskin earned his title of Champion by winning many first-place ribbons in dog shows. And he impressed the judges by more than his show performance. The prize poodle followed commands perfectly and was a handsome representative of his breed. But more than that, he seemed to know whether he had won or lost, before the judges announced their decision.

Whenever Rumpelstiltskin was sure he was going to be picked as the winner, he began wagging his tail and didn't stop until his name was announced. The proof that this was not just a lucky guess is that Rumpelstiltskin never wagged his tail before those few times he was not chosen for the top award. More than one judge waggishly remarked, "That poodle is doggone smart!"

3

Three Courageous Canines

Each year, a gold medal is awarded to a dog hero for outstanding bravery and devotion. For many years now, at an annual ceremony, some proud pooch is named National Dog Hero of the Year, and has an award slung around his or her neck. From all the stories of these courageous canines, here are three that show what it takes to be chosen Ken-L Ration's National Dog Hero of the Year.

Thumper

Thumper was still a clumsy-footed Saint Bernard puppy when he won his award in 1979. He lived with the Bodie family in Lockport, New York. Young as he was, Thumper knew his job — to look after three-year-old Benjamin Bodie. So, one morning when young Benji decided to go on a "tiger-hunting" expedition without telling any humans, Thumper went right along and stayed close to Benji's side.

The Bodie home was in farming country. It was fairly open land, but there were many ponds a small boy could fall into. There were rocks to stumble over, or perhaps conceal dangerous snakes. Benji was, of course, happily unaware of these real dangers. His "tiger hunt" took him farther and farther from home, and in an hour or so the boy and his dog had roamed a long way from the safety of the Bodies' front yard.

Later that morning, Benji's mother called to her son to give him a midmorning snack and discovered that the yard was deserted. Alarmed now, she called her husband. Together they searched the fields around the house, but they found not a trace of their son — or Thumper. At least the dog was with him, they thought.

Word of Benji's disappearance quickly spread, and very soon nearly a thousand searchers were combing the area. Twelve hours went by without a sign of the missing boy or his dog.

Night fell, making the difficult search many times harder. But the men and women kept going. Their lanterns and flashlights sent beams of light across the fields and woods, probing every spot where a small boy might be hidden.

At last, about two o'clock in the morning, some of the searchers heard barking off in the distance. Calling and listening for answering barks, they followed the sound until they came upon the excited pup. Thumper had been unwilling to leave his charge alone; instead, he yelped and barked to guide them to the small boy lying on the ground. But Benji didn't notice he had company; he was fast asleep. And although the night was chilly, he was warm. The dog hairs all over his clothing told the searchers that Thumper had stayed right next to him, warming him with his shaggy body until the rescuers got there.

When daylight came, Benji's parents traced the trail taken by the boy and his dog. "They came within a few feet of a pond," Mrs. Bodie said, "but Thumper had the good sense to stay with Benji and keep him out of the water. You don't expect such devotion from a puppy. He's our sweetheart!"

Thumper, the devoted Saint Bernard, was one of the youngest dogs ever to win the Dog Hero Award.

Chester to the Rescue

Chester was a Chesapeake Bay retriever who did more than share the Livingston, Montana, home of Mr. and Mrs. Gary Homme and five-year-old Kenny. Chester not only considered himself a full member of the family, he was also the Number One protector of the house and everyone who lived in it.

And so it was only natural that Chester would come to the rescue of Kenny, one cool spring day in 1978. The adventure began when Mrs. Homme looked out the kitchen window and saw that Kenny had vanished. Just moments before, he had been watering flowers in the garden. Could he have gone to the creek for more water?

Mrs. Homme rushed outside, just in time to hear her son shouting, "Help me! Mommy! Save me!"

Kenny had fallen down a steep hill not far from the house — and landed in the creek at the bottom of the hill. Ordinarily the creek was a gentle stream. But in the spring it was boiling with swift torrents of water rushing down from the mountains.

As Mrs. Homme hurried toward the creek, a furry torpedo zoomed past her. Seconds later, Chester's powerful body hit the water. But even as the dog swam toward Kenny, the raging flood pulled the boy into the mouth of a tunnel-like culvert.

Chester battled the water, inching closer and closer to Kenny. Then for ten minutes that seemed to last forever, Mrs. Homme looked on helplessly as the dog struggled to stay afloat near his master. Twice Kenny managed to dig his fingers into Chester's hair, but each time he lost his grip. Finally, Chester edged even closer, and Kenny was able to climb onto the dog's back. Together they swam to safety.

Mrs. Homme said gratefully when Chester received the gold medal as Dog Hero of 1978, "If we didn't have Chester, we wouldn't have a son now."

Meatball Means Safety

As you might expect, many German shepherds have received the Ken-L Ration Award as Dog Hero of the Year. This intelligent and loyal breed has a distinguished record among Seeing Eye dogs, war heroes, and family protectors. In 1977, Meatball, a German shepherd, upheld once again his breed's tradition of heroism.

Meatball lived with Mr. and Mrs. Robert Keith in Morris, Alabama. He was in the house one night when Mrs. Keith was home alone. She was talking on the phone when she heard someone pick up the extension phone in their greenhouse nearby. She knew it wasn't Mr. Keith. He was away on a trip. She felt all the more alone because there were no neighbors living close by whom she could call.

Mrs. Keith knew there was a gun in the house, but she decided she'd be even safer with her best weapon, Meatball. Together, they went to check out the greenhouse.

As she approached the darkened building, Mrs. Keith signaled Meatball to go on by himself. He moved silently through the darkness, stopping a few feet from the door, which was open. Inside, he could see a stranger. Meatball moved toward the door, growling.

The intruder was terrified at the menacing growls from the darkness. He dashed for the door and barely escaped the leaping German shepherd. With Meatball right on his heels, the would-be thief jumped into a waiting car. The man at the wheel gunned the motor, but before the thief could slam his door, Meatball lunged and grabbed his leg. With the ground scraping his belly, Meatball held on as the car gathered speed. The brave dog was dragged along the road until the thief finally kicked him loose.

Besides the bruises caused by the thief's kicks, Meatball suffered cuts on his paws, cracked toenails, and a badly scraped body. But to a proud protector like Meatball, it was a small price to pay for the appreciation of his family — and a gold medal around his neck.

4

The Phantom Hound of Yorkshire

Was it a real creature — or a phantom hound of heaven? The Reverend Isaac Woodcock was never sure....

Mr. Woodcock lived in Yorkshire, England, over a hundred years ago. He had a number of parishes and often had to travel by horseback or on foot over the open countryside. Sometimes he carried large amounts of money, collections from different churches to help support missions and take care of poor people.

The area where the clergyman lived was notorious for thieves and murderers, who preyed on the weak and helpless. But the Reverend Isaac Woodcock was neither weak nor helpless. He was not afraid of the men he called "the wicked doers of the devil's work," although many people thought he *should* be.

The night of February 6, 1854, seemed to be made for "the devil's work." It was bitterly cold and windy. Thick clouds rode the sky, and the pale moon shone fitfully.

On this winter's night, the good Mr. Woodcock was taking home two large sacks. One held important papers; the other held a large amount of money. He had strung the sacks across his shoulders by a heavy cord, and they bounced against his sides as he walked.

He was not armed. He was well protected, he said, "by the Good Book I carry with me everywhere." He kept it handy in his coat pocket.

As the fearless clergyman walked along the dark road, he quoted biblical verses to himself. It made the time pass more easily. A light snow began to fall. In the cloudy light, the silvery snow gave an eerie glow to the trees and shrubs on both sides of the road.

Mr. Woodcock heard an owl hoot close by. A moment later, the voice of another owl answered from deep in the surrounding woods. "At least," the clergyman told himself, "I think those are owls I hear."

Just then the clouds parted, and the landscape was bathed in brilliant moonlight. This was followed by a few seconds of silence. It was finally broken by the steady beat of footsteps. They were coming from somewhere behind the clergyman. The footsteps came faster and faster, closer and closer.

Mr. Woodcock stopped and wheeled around. "Who is there?" he called out.

And from out of a thin mist swirling behind him, a giant hound padded into the moonlight. It had a thick, uncombed coat of gray fur. It stood about level with the clergyman's chest, and he was a man well over six feet tall. But what captured his attention was the huge creature's eyes. They glowed with what he called "a white fire," like two small moons under a thin film of clouds.

This strange animal padded right up to the clergyman, but Mr. Woodcock was unafraid. He put out his hand to the dog, and the animal showed only friendliness. The large, rough tongue licked one of the clergyman's hands. At the same time, the dog turned its weird eyes up to stare at the man. They looked at each other for a long moment. Then, as if by agreement, they began to walk along the road. The dog stayed just to the right of the good man, never falling behind or going ahead.

Less than fifteen minutes passed, when the dog's behavior suddenly changed. It moved into the lead by several yards. Then, looking back as if to check on the clergyman's safety, it left the road and trotted along the shadowy line of maple trees.

All of a sudden the dog was gone, swallowed by the trees and darkness. Mr. Woodcock came to a halt, listening. There was no sound at all — not even the normal whistles and snapping twigs and other night sounds of birds and animals that are active in the dark hours. "It was a most unnatural silence," the clergyman said later. "It was as if I had entered another world."

Then the dog reappeared. Moving low to the ground, it came out of the woods and right up to the man. But it suddenly whirled toward the woods again and began to growl, a deep rumbling in its thick chest.

Now the clergyman heard a new sound. It was a brushing sound, such as clothing makes when it rubs against brush and branches. He turned in the direction it came from. As he did so, he caught a glimpse of three men slipping in and out of the shadows. The dog seemed rooted where it stood. It continued to growl menacingly at the spot where those men had been.

Mr. Woodcock patted the dog and started walking along the road again. It was growing late. His family would soon begin to worry about him. He didn't want them wandering about on a night like this, hunting for him.

Man and dog had traveled no more than another hundred yards when the deep growls started again. Again Mr. Woodcock searched in the direction the dog was facing. The moon was out now, and he saw, outlined against the sky, the same three men. They had come out of the woods and were standing farther down the road, waiting.

The dog leaped into a run, directly for the men. They broke for the cover of the trees. Soon the clergyman could hear branches cracking as they plunged deeper into the woods.

Mr. Woodcock caught up with the dog. "The quicker we get away from this place, the better," he said to his furry companion. And he set off at a good pace, the dog trotting alongside.

The would-be thieves were seen three more times by the clergyman as he made his way along the wooded path. Each time they seemed about to come at him. And one time he thought he saw weapons — guns and knives — in their hands. But each time they came out of hiding they were frightened off by Mr. Woodcock's growling guardian.

"However much they wanted the money at my side," the clergyman remarked, "they were not willing to risk the fury of my companion to come after it."

At long last, the walk ended as the clergyman reached his home. Standing just a few feet from the front door, Mr. Woodcock beckoned to the dog to come inside. "I will feed you," the man said.

The dog moved close to the clergyman. He licked the man's hand just the way he had before. He gazed at the man with those twin-moon eyes, barked softly one time — and vanished.

The Reverend Isaac Woodcock told the events of that fantastic night again and again, until the end of his life. He believed firmly that it had all happened just the way he remembered it. He talked to everyone who lived within several miles of his home, asking about the phantom of the night. Nobody knew of such an animal. Not one person had ever seen or heard about a dog anything like that one.

They were sure that the clergyman's life — and

the church's money — had been saved that night by a supernatural creature. In time, the clergyman came to share their feelings. And every time he walked the road that wound through the dark woods, he kept a sharp lookout for his phantom friend. The dog never reappeared. But then, Mr. Woodcock was never again followed by thieves!

5

The Shopping Basket Beagle

Once, dogs were trained to beg on the street corner for their owners. Dogs today delight in carrying their owners' packages. This is the story of a pet beagle who put both tricks to good use — out of love for his mistresses in distress.

Joanne and Jeanne Burgess were elderly twins who lived in Philadelphia, Pennsylvania, about fifty years ago. Before they retired, both sisters had worked in the neighborhood library for many years. To all the library users they had been unfailingly kind, helpful, and patient; and they were especially well-liked by the young people.

The two sisters shared a small apartment, living on money they had saved over the years and on a small retirement income. Then trouble struck. First one sister, and then the other, became ill. The doctor bills were high, and their savings were soon gone.

When the Burgess sisters finally recovered, they had only their tiny retirement income to live on. They spent little on food, and that included a few cents a day for food for Shakespeare, their seven-year-old beagle.

Winter came early that year of 1935. The sisters stayed indoors most of the time, huddled in their chilly living room. Shakespeare kept them company. His place was on the rug between their chairs. But every so often he would get up and poke his nose into the hand of one sister or the other, and be rewarded with a gentle pat.

Before their illness, Joanne and Jeanne used to play with their pet. They would throw a ball for him to fetch, or teach him new tricks. One of his favorite tricks was to go into the kitchen and bring back a wicker basket. Carrying it gently in his mouth, by the handle, he would proudly take it to one of the sisters, who would drop in a dog biscuit. Shakespeare would then take his "shopping basket" back to the kitchen, put it down, and eat his snack.

Christmas was coming, but there was no money to buy even a box of snacks for Shakespeare. In fact, there was not enough money to pay for the rent, electricity, and so on — and still have money left for food.

One day, Shakespeare went to the apartment door and scratched, as he did when he wanted to go for a walk. But when one of the sisters put on her coat to take him out, Shakespeare refused to go. After a while, the sisters realized that Shakespeare wanted to go out by himself.

So one of them went downstairs with him and opened the front door. Shakespeare stayed in the street for about five minutes and came back, scratching at the front door. The sister let him in, and they went back upstairs.

For several days, one of the sisters let him out, then in again a few minutes later. Then one afternoon Shakespeare went into the kitchen, returned with his shopping basket, and stood in front of the door. He wanted to go out with the basket. Joanne laughed.

"Why not let him play his game?" she said, smiling. "What harm can there be in it?"

"Of course," said Jeanne, smiling also. "Why, he can even go shopping for us."

This amused Joanne. She gazed down at Shakespeare and said, "Now, go to the bakery and bring back some bread. We can also use eggs and vegetables."

"And while you are there," Jeanne added, "don't forget some treats for yourself."

Patting Shakespeare's head, Joanne opened the door. She walked behind him down the stairs and let him out the front door.

"Don't be gone too long," she said, as if speaking to a young boy or girl.

Shakespeare did not come back in five minutes. When ten minutes had passed, Joanne began to worry. She opened the door and stepped outside. The wind was raw and biting. The brown-and-white dog was nowhere in sight. She called his name, but there was no sign of Shakespeare; she hurried upstairs and told Jeanne what had happened.

While they were talking, Jeanne looked anxiously out the front window. Shakespeare was out there, somewhere. Was he all right? Fat snowflakes were fluttering down, whirling in the wind. Soon the ground was white with snow.

It was just beginning to grow dark when Joanne thought she heard a dog barking. She went to the window and looked down. There stood Shakespeare, the basket on the snowy ground between his front paws. He barked again. Joanne tapped on the window to let him know she was on her way. Then she happily went downstairs to let him in.

Shakespeare did not wait to be petted. With the basket held firmly in his mouth, he trotted past Joanne and up the stairs. On the landing, he waited for the apartment door to be opened. Joanne was so pleased to have Shakespeare back that she didn't even notice the newspaper covering the top of the basket. She quickly opened the door and let the dog inside. Jeanne was waiting to greet him.

Jeanne saw the newspaper right away. After petting the wet and shivering beagle and rubbing him dry with a towel, she said, "Did you bring us something to read? Well, that was a very nice thing to do."

"Yes, thank you," said Joanne. She reached down and lifted the newspaper off the basket.

"Oh, my goodness!" gasped Jeanne. Her sister was speechless as she stared at the basket.

Shakespeare's eyes went from one sister to the other. Then he nudged the basket with his nose.

He seemed to be saying, "Here, take it. I brought it back for you."

Jeanne bent down, lifted the heavy basket, and set it on a table. Then she took out, one by one, the things resting in it. A loaf of fresh bread. A jar of strawberry jam. Milk. Cheese. Carrots. Crisp apples. And a box of dog treats for Shakespeare.

The sisters were shocked. They could not imagine how this had happened. Did Shakespeare take somebody's basket while that person was shopping? Did he grab it from the hand of a shopper on the way home from the store? And how did the newspaper get on top of the food?

Finally, Jeanne turned the newspaper over and found a note clipped to the underside, where the snow could not wet it.

Jeanne read the note to her sister: "'You gave us so much for so long. Now let us give you a little to thank you!'"

"Oh, my," she said, wiping her eyes. "And, Joanne, it is signed, 'All your friends from the library.'"

When the two sisters had recovered, they quickly dressed and went to the local stores. They knew every one of the store-owners. They had met most of them as children just starting to use the neighborhood library. But at each store they were given answers like, "No, we have no idea who put food in Shakespeare's basket." And, "Maybe it was Santa Claus. After all, this is the season for giving, isn't it?"

The sisters went home, puzzled but grateful for the much-needed food. That evening they ate well, and Shakespeare enjoyed a saucer of milk to wash down his dessert of dog treats.

The next day, Shakespeare went out with his shopping basket. He again returned with food in it. More milk. A bag of rolls. A piece of ham and four lamb chops. And a meaty bone for Shakespeare. Along with the food came another note. This one said, "Merry Christmas — and a wonderful New Year!"

And a wonderful new year it was for Jeanne and Joanne and their pet beagle. Thanks to Shakespeare, the friends they had made over fifty years were able to help. They would not let the twins go hungry or lack for anything. Whatever the sisters needed, their friends made sure they got. It was a shower of love for all the kindness, helpfulness, and patience the two sisters had given their neighbors through the years. And, the store-owners agreed, there was no finer delivery dog than Shakespeare, known all over Philadelphia as "The Shopping Basket Beagle."

6

The Great Dog Robbery!

Stealing valuable dogs and other pets for ransom or resale has been a crime for centuries. It is not often, though, that a respectable businessman steals from an emperor to meet the demands of his country's leading citizens! This is what happened in the following story about two Pekingese, Ah Cum and Mimosa.

Pekingese dogs have lived in China for almost 3,000 years, but not until 1860 did a Westerner first see the "sacred lion dog" of the Chinese imperial court. That happened during a war between China, and England and France.

A combined force of French and British troops captured China's imperial city of Peking. While they were searching the Imperial Palace, some of the soldiers found five strange, tiny dogs huddled together, far back in the deserted palace grounds.

Dogs are especially prized by Englishmen, and the highest-ranking British officer immediately took charge of the tiny, fluffy dogs with the pug noses. A few days later, the five Pekingese were sent to England by ship to be given as special gifts. One was presented to Queen Victoria. The other four were given to two noble English families, a male and a female to each.

It didn't take long before the first litter of puppies was born. And within a few years, the homes of many wealthy English families were echoing to the shrill barks of Pekingese puppies.

After a while, though, the rage to own a Pekingese died down. One reason was that so few of the little dogs looked like the original Pekingese from China. Not enough care was being taken in their breeding, and dog-lovers were getting worricd about the future for all Pekes. One Englishman, Alfred de Rothschild, wrote a letter to the emperor of China, asking if the emperor would consider selling some of the sacred lion dogs.

"Not one of our much-loved dogs is for sale," came the answer. "And His Highness has asked me to inform you that these dogs are closely guarded at all times. Anyone caught trying to steal them will be punished most severely. By torture, certainly ... even death!"

This seemed to end any hope of bringing better Pekingese to England. But a British businessman, Douglas Murray, saw a way to make some money for himself — selling the dogs at a high price — and doing English dog-lovers a favor at the same time.

Mr. Murray's scheme was possible because he traded with Chinese merchants regularly. He made secret arrangements to have two of the palace pets stolen, then smuggled out of China.

"Murray was willing to offer a high price for this service," wrote one historian. "Of course, if the thief failed in his attempts, all Mr. Murray stood to lose was some money. The thief, however, would most likely lose his life."

Luck was with the thief and Mr. Murray. Two dogs — one a male named Ah Cum, the other a female named Mimosa — were smuggled out of

China. The Pekingese were placed in a box of hay, which was then hidden in a large wooden crate. Along with the dogs in the crate was a Japanese deer, which further camouflaged the stolen treasures.

Ah Cum and Mimosa were perfect models of their breed. The puppies born to them were just as beautiful and perfectly formed. And for almost a hundred years since then, Pekingese breeders have worked hard to produce puppies equal to the perfect pair, Ah Cum and Mimosa.

So the next time you see one of these little dogs — they stand about six inches high and weigh about nine pounds — be very respectful. After all, Pekingese are 3,000-year-old, sacred lion dogs, highly prized by royalty, and brought to the West, not legally, but at great risk and cost.

7

The Dog with the Super Sense

Some people know when a thing is going to happen before it actually occurs. Do dogs also have a "sixth sense?" Read this story, then decide.

Candy, a Boston terrier, was devoted to her young master, twelve-year-old Paul Burns of New Orleans, Louisiana. She would have liked to follow him to school, but Paul's mother made sure

Candy was inside when Paul left the house each morning. Candy seemed to understand that this separation would last only until Paul came home in the afternoon.

So Paul and his mother thought it was very odd, one rainy March morning, when Candy began jumping up and down in front of the door as Paul picked up his books and got ready to leave the house.

"Stop that, Candy!" Paul's mother said in a stern voice. "Come here!"

Candy would not move away from the door. And when Paul reached for the doorknob, her barking and excitement increased. Then, bunching her little black-and-white body into a tight ball, Candy jumped so high, she batted the books out of Paul's arms; they fell to the floor with a crash.

"Something's really wrong, Mom," Paul said. "Candy wouldn't act like this unless she had a real good reason."

"Maybe so," Mrs. Burns answered. "But you have to get to school, and —"

Her words were cut short by a flash of light and a loud *crack!* from outside the house, then a deafening crash of thunder. Paul and his mother rushed to a window and peered out. There on the lawn, a few feet from the front walk, stood what remained of their big old oak tree. The trunk was split, and ribbons of smoke were drifting up from it. A bolt of lightning had struck and destroyed the great tree.

"Mom, that's where I would have been walking," Paul said in a whisper, "if Candy hadn't kept me inside."

His mother nodded. "She must have felt the electricity in the air. Dogs are more sensitive than people to things like that. It frightened her, made her act in a crazy way."

Paul shook his head as he knelt to stroke Candy's head. "I don't think so, Mom. I think she *knew* what was going to happen."

Was it the electricity in the air that Candy felt? Electric storms are not rare in New Orleans, Louisiana, where Paul lived. Candy had experienced them before. But she had never acted in this way. Paul was always sure Candy knew, by some sixth sense, that he was in immediate danger and had done all she could to protect him.

8

Missy's Marvelous Journey

"He is such a good pal he would go to the ends of the earth for his friends," is sometimes said about very special people — and dogs, too — dogs like the famous Lassie of screen and story. The canine pal in this story was an actual dog, a chow named Missy, who lived in Kansas.

The year was 1933; the country was in the midst of the Great Depression. Millions of people were out of work and out of money to feed themselves and their families. Nowhere was it worse than in Kansas.

Missy's owner, Jacob Zanger, had just lost his farm to the bank because he could not keep up the payments on his mortgage. Now, with only a few dollars left, Mr. Zanger decided it was time to pack up and get out. He'd take his family of five farther west, searching for work along the way.

It was hard for the children to leave the place

where they'd lived all their lives. It was even harder to leave when their father told them that Missy, their dog, would have to be left behind. The children had petted and fed her, romped with her, and wrestled with her since she was a puppy. They couldn't understand that their parents did not even have the little money it took to feed a dog.

Missy was given to a neighbor. The children cried and cried as they drove west. But all too soon the car had left Kansas far behind.

From the first, Missy's new owner couldn't stop her from running back to the farm. Each morning the chow would go to the deserted Zanger house, searching for her family. And each night, Missy's new owner would come and bring her back. This went on for a week. Then one day Missy disappeared for good.

Almost a year went by. In that time Mr. Zanger had found work in Monterey, California, and the Zangers were living in a house there. The children still pined so much for Missy that their mother and father told them to find another dog. The children shook their heads, and the oldest said, "We don't want a dog if we can't have Missy."

Mr. Zanger scratched his head, trying to understand. "I'm sorry about leaving Missy back in Kansas. We just had no way of feeding her. Now we can feed a dog — and you don't want one." He sighed. "I can't figure you kids out."

Just four days later, as the youngest Zanger child was walking home from school, a dirty, scruffy dog came running at him. The little boy cringed away. The gaunt, wild-eyed dog with the matted coat frightened him.

The boy tried to get away. It was no use. The dog caught up to him and leaped against his chest, knocking him to the ground. The boy threw a protective hand across his face — barely in time to stop the dog's tongue from washing his nose. The wet tongue got past the hand to the boy's chin . . . cheeks . . . ears . . .

The young Zanger boy looked through his fingers and saw a furry tail wagging. He felt the dog's kisses. And suddenly he heard his older sister yelling, "Missy! It's Missy. She's home!"

The chow's love for the Zanger family was so strong that the dog had found her way over fifteen hundred miles to be with them. Somehow this medium-sized, homebody pet had tracked down her family in spite of all the dangerous highways, deserts, mountains, and towns she had to travel. She was exhausted, the pads of her feet were torn, and she was half-starved. But she had reached her goal.

Just what had happened to Missy on her ten-month journey, and how she was able to follow the trail of a car all those miles, will always be a mystery. But there was no mystery about *why* she did it. Her kisses said it all.

9

Professor Ueno's Faithful Friend

In every country stories are told of dogs' loyalty and devotion to their human friends. In Japan, people tell about Hachiko. Because of Hachiko, hundreds of dog-lovers meet once a year to hold a special ceremony at a railroad station in Tokyo, Japan.

The story begins on a June day in 1920. A short, thin man is walking along a crowded street in

Tokyo. He is Dr. Ueno, a professor at Tokyo University. Walking at his side is his pet, Hachiko. The dog is an Akita, a popular breed in Japan.

People smile at the professor and his dog. Hachiko is not yet a year old, and he still frisks and bounces like a puppy. Dr. Ueno returns the smiles of the people, sharing their good feelings about his playful companion.

The man and his dog reach the railway station. There they will part. Dr. Ueno must take a train out to the university, where he will spend the day. Hachiko is already used to this — they have been coming to the station together for a month now.

Hachiko waits to be petted by Dr. Ueno. Then he trots to an out-of-the-way place on the station platform. He watches the professor get on the train. When it pulls out of the station and disappears down the track, Hachiko stretches out on the floor. This is what Dr. Ueno called "Hachiko's waiting place."

All day long, Hachiko stays at the station. Once in a while he will get up and move around. But he does not wander far, and he always returns to the same spot. This is how he spends the hours of each day — waiting for Dr. Ueno to come home. In the evening, near the time when the professor's train will pull into the station, Hachiko sits up, looking bright and alert, facing the direction the train will come from.

As soon as the train stops, Hachiko bounds across the platform. Dr. Ueno steps down to be greeted by barks and a wet tongue. Dr. Ueno pets his loving dog, says a few kind words, and they start their walk home. It is, Dr. Ueno said, Hachiko's "golden time of day."

Hachiko never failed to be there when his master got off the train. The people at the station liked to talk about Hachiko. They decided that the professor must be a kind and loving person to bring out such devotion from his pet. They were right. Professor Ueno was very good to Hachiko; the dog led a happy, healthy life. And for years, these morning and evening scenes at the station were repeated daily.

Finally, however, on an evening in the spring of 1925, Professor Ueno did not get off the evening train. Hachiko waited, but his master did not arrive on later trains, either. Some neighbors of Professor Ueno tried to get the dog to go home with them, but Hachiko would not leave. Not until late at night did he give up his vigil and walk home alone.

Maybe Hachiko thought he would find the professor at home, that he had somehow missed him.

But Professor Ueno would never come home again. He had died that afternoon, at the university. Hachiko was fed by the housekeeper. After that, the dog paced through the house, sniffing in corners, returning again and again to the professor's bedroom. At last, whining softly, Hachiko fell asleep near Dr. Ueno's bed.

The next morning, Hachiko left the house the same time as always. He walked to the station, found his "waiting place," and stretched out on the floor. . . .

That evening, and every evening for the next nine years, Hachiko faithfully followed the same routine. He waited for all the passengers to get off the train. Only when it was clear that Dr. Ueno was not coming did Hachiko leave the station and walk home.

The vigil did not end until March, 1934, nine years after Dr. Ueno's death. And when Hachiko did not show up for several days, some people wondered why. One of them called a newspaper reporter, asking him to find out what had happened to Hachiko. Soon the story of the dog who was loyal till the day he died was told in the Japanese newspapers.

Hundreds of people were deeply moved by the story. And when one newspaper suggested that a statue of Hachiko should be placed in his "wait-ing place," contributions poured in. Not only did money come from Japanese readers, it came from dog-lovers all over the world, including the United States.

With this money, a handsome bronze statue of Hachiko was set up in Tokyo's Shibuya Station, at a ceremony where "friends of Hachiko" recalled stories of the dog's steadfast devotion.

Many years have passed since then. But the statue still stands in Hachiko's "waiting place," a reminder of a loyalty that was stronger than death.

10

The Dog Who Directed Traffic

Dogs, in their role of protector, often play babysitter to the small children in their family. But few dogs have attempted to control traffic to protect them....

Ringo, a large mutt with a ring of thick white fur around his neck, won the Ken-L Ration Gold Medal as Dog Hero of the Year for his *traffic direction.*

Ringo had found himself an orphan in Texas when he was much too young to fend for himself. He tried begging at the Salehs' door before Christmas, and Mrs. Saleh chased him away. Later, though, when she discovered him in the garage trying to eat a mop because he was so hungry, she couldn't bear it. She took him inside and fed him until he was full and sleepy.

There wasn't a big hassle about keeping him. The Salehs had four children, one of them a baby, and they liked dogs. In fact, they had planned to get a beagle for Christmas, but the children decided that Ringo was just what they wanted.

The dog, part Saint Bernard, grew and grew, until he could hold a full-grown man at bay if he had wanted to. Mostly, he played with Randy, now two and a half years old, and traveled with the little boy. Randy was a great traveler.

One day, shortly before Randy's father was to install a gate in the fence to keep his son from roaming so much, Randy disappeared. Usually, his family would find him wandering around the empty lots of the town. But this time both Randy and Ringo had vanished. Two hours later there was still no sign of them.

These two may have moved fast, but down on Pipeline Road traffic was at a standstill. A long line of cars stretched down the road from a sharp, blind curve.

Harley Jones, a school maintenance man, got tired of waiting for the forty cars in front of him to move. He got out and walked ahead to see what was causing the delay.

A motorist in a car he passed warned him about a "mad dog in the street." Jones decided he had to see this with his own eyes. He hesitated as he got near the curve. Then, as he rounded it, he stared in amazement.

Stationed in the middle of the road was a huge dog. It was Ringo. If a car attempted to move, he

49

would leap at it, snarling and barking. It was as if he had decided this was his territory and no car could enter it. Mystified, Jones took a few steps nearer and saw, beyond the curve, a little boy playing in the middle of the heavily traveled roadway. It was Randy.

The dog would leave his traffic post every few minutes to try and nudge Randy to the side of the road. But Randy decided it was a great game. He would immediately run back to the center and sit there, laughing.

Jones could see that the dog was almost exhausted. Each time Ringo ran back to keep the traffic at bay, Jones moved a little nearer to the child. He was afraid to move quickly. The dog's protective instincts were so aroused that he was growling and snapping at Jones. He even stood between Jones and Randy until a car summoned him back to traffic duty.

By inching his way and talking soothingly to the dog, Jones finally managed to reach the child, pick him up, and carry him to the side of the road, with Ringo growling at Jones, all the while. But once Jones reached the side of the road, Ringo relaxed. When the first car appeared around the curve, the dog didn't give it a glance. His traffic duty was over. Randy, his charge, was safe.

11

The Dog Who Changed History

A scientist's dog may actually have set scientific discoveries back by decades. This is what happened one night, more than three hundred years ago....

Sir Isaac Newton (who discovered the law of gravity when an apple fell on his head) was a brilliant mathematician. He was working late one night in his library on some new mathematical theories. His devoted dog, Diamond, was sleeping nearby.

Hearing a knock at the front door, Sir Isaac went to answer it and closed the library door behind him. On the table at which he had been working were important papers. He had written down new ideas and mathematical computations — ideas and formulas he had been working on for years. Also on that table was a burning candle, the light by which he worked.

Although Sir Isaac had closed the door quietly,

Diamond woke up and was instantly alert. The dog could hear his master talking with someone at the front door, and he wanted to be sure he was safe. He tried to go to his master but couldn't because the door was firmly shut.

Diamond grew frantic. He raced around the room, barking. In his excitement he accidentally struck a table leg and jarred the candle loose. It fell on the table, setting fire to Sir Isaac's papers. Fortunately, the fire was discovered before much damage was done to the library. But it was too late to save the valuable papers.

Many a master would have been furious with such a "stupid animal" for having destroyed years of work and precious ideas that could change the way man thought. But Sir Isaac knew his dog. Diamond had just been frantic with worry about his master's safety when he caused the accident. And that is why the great scientist said only, "Alas, little Diamond, you cannot know how much harm your moment of excitement has caused." Then he petted the dog and went to bed, his mind busily trying to recall the ideas and numbers now gone up in smoke.

12

Two Hunters Take the Trail

The Royal Canadian Mounted Police are world-famous for "always getting their man." They are proud of their record, but they are quick to share it with some very reliable members of their detective force — the K-9 division. The RCMP has been using dogs for tracking since it began its K-9 program back in the 1930's. These dogs and their handlers are on call at all times of the day or night.

Different kinds of dogs have been members of the RCMP, but the German shepherd breed is generally favored because it is hardworking, strong, brave, and deeply loyal.

A call came into RCMP Headquarters in Cloverdale, near Vancouver, British Columbia, on the afternoon of January 13, 1955. "There's been a holdup," the caller said, "at the Burnaby branch of the Royal Bank of Canada. Can you send some help out here, and maybe one of your K-9 dogs?"

A huge police hunt was already in progress when the Mountie and his dog, a German shepherd, arrived at the bank. A bank teller came up to them and said, "I saw them drive off in their car, heading out of town."

One of the bandits had torn his pants during the escape. The piece of cloth, found on the sidewalk outside the bank, was held to the nose of Silver, the four-footed hunter. She sniffed the cloth. Then she put her nose in the air, sniffed again, and pulled at the leash held by her handler.

"She's picked up the scent," the Mountie said. "Silver, let's see if you can take us to those men."

The dog trotted off, stopping now and then to check the trail. Within an hour she had led her handler and several officers into the countryside outside the town. The sun was starting to set, but Silver's sharp sense of smell would be all they needed to follow a trail in the dark. And a moment later she began moving faster, as if the end of the trail was near.

"Hold it," called another policeman, catching up to Silver and her handler. "The holdup men were just captured. Less than a mile from here, in the direction you're going."

Silver had been hot on the trail and closing in. It was clear that she would have finished the job if several Mounties hadn't found the robbers' hideout first.

"But don't let the trail get cold," added the other policeman. "We didn't find any of the money they stole. See if she can come up with that."

Silver put her nose back to work. In a short while she paused over an overcoat lying on the ground. It was later found to belong to one of the holdup men. Now, with this fresh scent to go on, the K-9 sleuth hurried along through the fields and into a small wooded area. About twenty minutes later she had led her handler to a plastic bag, hidden behind a tree. The bag was stuffed with cash. It was part of the loot stolen from the bank, and a count showed it to be more than $15,000.

Silver stayed on the trail and soon zeroed in on another bag. This one had $2,000 in it. On and on she sniffed, finding one bag after another. Before the night ended, Silver and her handler had recovered over $27,000 in stolen currency. Only $98.00 of the missing money failed to turn up.

Silver made headlines for her fantastic work, and the Royal Bank of Canada gave her a fine collar with an inscription, praising the RCMP dog for her role in tracking the holdup men and finding the stolen money. As one of the bank officers put it, "Silver is worth her weight in gold!"

Just about one year later, on January 16, 1956, another K-9 dog became a Canadian hero. This was a male dog, named Duke, who put his nose to the trail in a desperate hunt for three missing boys.

The call for help came late in the afternoon. The young boys, ranging in age from eight to ten, had last been seen near the entrance to an abandoned coal mine near Sydney Forks, Nova Scotia. They had been gone since sometime that morning. Searchers had scoured the area around the mine and inside, but they could find no trace of the missing trio.

Duke and his handler investigated the ground near the mine entrance. Ten minutes ... fifteen minutes — then Duke tugged hard on the leash. He wanted to go into the main tunnel of the mine.

The dog, his handler, and six other men were lowered almost fifty feet into the tunnel. They turned on portable lamps and began to move deeper into the mine. They looked for signs that the boys had been there. Every now and then they called the boys' names. But there was no answer.

The air got worse and worse the farther they went. It was dark and hard to breathe. At last the thin air made the lamps go out. And the searchers came up against another problem when they reached a network of tunnels. The passages fanned out in a dozen different directions.

The hunters split up into search parties of one or two men. Duke was most interested in following the main shaft, so he and his handler went that way. They edged into the blackness, the handler relying on Duke to decide which direction they should take and how fast they should move. It seemed as if they had gone miles (it turned out to be just a quarter-mile) when Duke pulled the Mountie into one of the side tunnels.

The man took a few stumbling steps, then heard a gasp. He squinted, trying to see into the darkness. "What is it, Duke?" he said.

"It's us, mister!" a voice whispered from close by. "We got lost. Thank God you found us."

The Mountie dropped to his knees. He could barely see the boy who was talking to him. He put a comforting hand on the boy's shoulder. "I didn't find you, son. It was Duke. But I'm sure glad he did!"

The dog's bark echoed in the dark tunnel, sending an "okay" signal to the other searchers. Duke could sense the happiness of his handler and the relief and joy of the three boys. They were tired, but the fear that had gripped them for hours disappeared step by step as Duke and the Mountie led them to fresh air and safety, and a welcome from the other searchers.

There were some very relieved and thankful families in Sydney Forks that night. And they owed their thanks — and the lives of three children — to the educated nose of a dog named Duke.

13

The Dog Who Wouldn't Give Up

Dogs have gone to war along with their masters, from early times. This story goes back about two hundred years.

Corporal Burat was a soldier in Napoleon's army. Not a combat soldier fighting with rifle and sword, but a flag-bearer. It was Burat's duty to carry the flag of his regiment into battle, and to keep it flying until the battle was over. The flag was important to the soldiers. Defeat seemed impossible as long as they could see it flying.

Burat was proud of his assignment, and he took great care of the flag.

The French corporal always had his dog at his side when he went into battle. The dog was a mongrel named White Paw, and as true to Burat as Burat was to his flag. Both their loyalties were tested heavily one day, when the forces of France met those of Portugal, England, and Spain in battle.

As the two armies hammered at each other, Burat was knocked to earth by a charging horse, and the flagpole was ripped from his hand and broken. Burat jumped to his feet, grabbed the part of the pole still attached to the flag and, with his other hand, wielded his sword. He accounted for three fallen enemy soldiers before a blow from a saber sent him sprawling.

While Burat lay on the ground, an enemy soldier snatched up the flag. But White Paw hurled herself at the soldier and was biting his hand when her master regained consciousness. Burat staggered over and grabbed back the flag. The Portuguese soldier was glad to let it go. By this time, he'd had enough; he stumbled away.

Burat raised the flag, only to be struck again by an enemy soldier. He fell, wounded. Another Portuguese soldier tried to capture the flag, but White Paw would not let him touch it. The man was bleeding from a dozen bites before he finally gave up and ran off.

White Paw licked her master's face until he opened his eyes. The battle had ended, and the flag — torn and spattered with mud — lay by Burat's side. He petted White Paw, thanking her for being so brave and dependable.

And that is when Burat saw her wound. A

sword had made a long, deep slash along her side. She was bleeding, but she would not whine or lick the wound while Burat needed her help.

The French soldier carried White Paw to a nearby stream. Finding a shirt on the ground, he tore it into strips and, after wetting them, bound White Paw's wound. Then, weak from his own loss of blood, Burat fainted.

When he woke up, Burat found he had been captured by the enemy. He had been taken behind their lines, where a doctor had treated his wounds. The doctor, who was English, told Burat, "As soon as you are well enough to travel, you will be taken to England."

White Paw was still with him, and Burat asked, "Can I take my dog with me? She saved my life."

The doctor was sorry, but he told Burat that no dogs would be allowed aboard ship. Burat was saddened, and he asked the doctor to look after White Paw.

The next day the Frenchman was marched aboard the ship, one of a number of prisoners of war bound for an English jail. But just as they were sailing out of the harbor, Burat looked back and saw with horror that White Paw was swimming after the ship! She was still wearing the bandage he had put on her wound.

"Go back!" Burat cried, fearful that the dog would drown.

But White Paw swam on. The distance between dog and ship was growing wider. Burat knew she would not give up and that she would certainly drown if he did not do something. Pushing aside an English soldier, he dived into the sea.

Burat could hear the shouts behind him as he swam to meet White Paw. She could barely stay afloat, and he held her head up, treading water, as he watched a small boat being lowered from the ship. A short while later the boat drew alongside, and two British sailors reached out to bring him aboard.

"I will not enter your boat," Burat said defiantly, "unless my dog comes with me."

There was no doubt that Burat meant what he said. Finally, both man and dog were pulled from the water.

Burat and White Paw were taken to England, where they went to jail together. It is not known how White Paw helped her master in this situation, but it is a fact that Burat and his dog escaped from the prison. They managed to cross to the seacoast town of Dunkirk, France. From there, they found their way back to Burat's regiment.

Soon after their arrival, Burat was given a new flag to carry into battle. And White Paw was given a rousing cheer by all the men of the regiment.

It was an unforgettable moment for the corporal and the dog who would never give up.

14

Pedro Amaro's Devil Dog

If his master is wronged, will his dog seek justice?

In 1914, in Mexico, government troops captured Pedro Amaro, a soldier in the bandit army of the famous Mexican chief, Pancho Villa.

When Amaro was taken prisoner, a small black dog was found hiding in the cave with him. The officer in charge of the troops was going to shoot the dog, but Amaro pleaded for his pet's life. Amigo (which means "friend" in Spanish) was spared.

Pedro and Amigo were taken back to Mexico City. There, the dog was told to "go home," and Pedro was put in prison. He was soon tried and found guilty of being a traitor to the Mexican government. His sentence was a life behind bars.

Even so, Amaro's friends and family felt that Pedro was lucky. He could have been sentenced to die. Now, at least, there was a chance that he might be freed after serving time for being a rebel. And there was also the hope of freedom if Pancho Villa won his war against the federal troops.

Pedro's sister often visited her brother in the prison. Once, she took the dog with her. Amigo had to wait outside the wall. But he was able to look up and see Pedro waving to him from a window. Now he knew at least that his master was alive. He whined softly, wanting to be with the man he loved.

Every day Amigo was fed by Pedro's sister. And every night the little black dog would go to the prison. He would sit on the ground below Pedro's window, watching for any sign of his master.

This went on for more than a month. At least once each evening, Pedro would come to the window and call out to the dog. But then, one night,

Pedro did not appear. Amigo stayed until the sun came up, then wandered home.

This happened the next night and the night after that. Pedro's family and friends saw how the dog was acting, and they wondered why. The answer came on the third day. Six men had murdered Pedro in prison. They were to go on trial for the crime.

These six men hated Pancho Villa and any man who served in his army. Villa's soldiers had killed relatives of three of the six. And the other three prisoners also had personal reasons to hate the famous bandit, who was a hero to many Mexicans. Because Pedro was a loyal follower of Pancho Villa, they had taken his life. It was, they told a jury, the only way they could get revenge.

The trial was over quickly. The six guilty men would pay for the crime with their lives. They would be hanged, a punishment that would also be a warning to all other prisoners with revenge on their minds.

The day after the trial ended something strange happened. Amigo, who had stopped coming to the prison after Pedro's death, began to come again. Each night he would sit under Pedro's window and howl for almost an hour. The guards would chase him away. But as soon as they were back inside the gates, Amigo would return and start to howl again. He would stop at exactly midnight.

Soon everyone was talking about the strange black dog — the guards, the prisoners, Pedro's family and friends. How, they asked, did Amigo know his master had been murdered at midnight? Yet he had to know. Why else would he howl that way, then stop at exactly the moment the church bells began to toll the midnight hour?

Then something even stranger happened. For the first time, Amigo visited the prison while the sun was still shining. It was on the afternoon that the first murderer of Pedro Amaro was to be hanged.

Amigo sat in his usual place outside the stone wall. He looked directly at the window where Pedro used to appear. Inside, on the other side of the wall, there was the sound of marching feet. The soldiers were bringing the prisoner to be hanged. Then there was the murmur of voices. After that came a loud noise, followed by a moment of silence. The execution was over.

Only now was Amigo ready to go. He got up and walked home slowly.

The little black dog returned for each of the hangings. And until the last one was over, Amigo showed up each night and howled until the bells of midnight tolled over the city.

There were whispers that Amigo had in him the soul of Pedro Amaro. And there were other whispers that he was a messenger of the devil. Still others said that Amigo was sent by the forces of good, not evil.

No one will ever know why Amigo's final visit to the prison came on the day that the last of the six murderers was hanged. But Pedro's sister was sure that Amigo had stood by to see justice done, and that now her brother was finally at peace.

15

Marvelous Rolf,
the Counting Dog

A dog that can count, and add and subtract, and answer questions with "words"? Rolf stumped the scientists....

In Germany, in 1914, an Irish terrier named Rolf lived with Madame Moekel, her husband, and her daughter in the city of Mannheim. Rolf had always been a clever dog. He learned to obey commands soon after he was born. He would sit, stay,

turn over, shake hands, and do even more compli-
cated tricks. But he would take orders only from
Madame Moekel.

One afternoon Madame Moekel and Frieda,
her daughter, were sitting at the kitchen table,
where Madame Moekel was trying to give Frieda
a lesson in arithmetic. Rolf was watching them
intently. It was a lovely spring day, and Frieda
was more interested in playing outside with her
friends than in learning how to add and subtract.

"Come, come," her mother said, beginning to
lose patience. "You must get this right. Then you
can play. Now, how much are two and four?"

Frieda twisted a curl of her blond hair around a
finger. She stared blankly at her mother for a moment. Then she said, "Five?"

The woman sighed heavily. As she did, Rolf
came over and put both of his front paws on the
table. He looked right at Frieda. Then he raised
one paw and slapped it down on the table. He
raised the paw again and brought it down in the
same way. He did this six times, barked at
Madame Moekel, and dropped down again on all
four feet.

The woman and her daughter were amused —
and amazed! Madame Moekel hurried next door
to get her neighbors to see this astounding feat.

"Watch and listen," Madame Moekel told

them. Then she asked Frieda the same arithmetic question. Again Frieda said, "Five," and again Rolf put his paws on the table and slapped it six times.

The two old women smiled at Madame Moekel. "Your dog is very smart," one of them said. "He is clever to have learned that trick from you. Now we must get back to our cooking."

"Wait! You do not understand," Rolf's mistress said. "I did not teach Rolf this trick. He learned it all by himself."

One of the women frowned at Madame Moekel. "Well, then, let us see if he also learned to add three and five," she said.

Madame Moekel called the dog to her. He trotted up to her side at once. "Now," she asked him, "how much are three and five?"

The terrier barked twice and put his paws against the edge of the table. He barked once more, then slapped the wood eight times without stopping.

This time the neighbors were impressed and took turns testing Rolf. But he would not answer unless Madame Moekel put the question to him. Each problem they set required simple addition, and he gave his mistress the correct answer to each one.

Word soon spread all over town. Rolf was

described as a wonder dog. Three professors from a local school were sent to the house to test Rolf. He passed their addition test with perfect marks — so long as Madame Moekel asked the questions.

One of the professors took Madame Moekel aside. "I want you to do it another way," he told her. "Stand outside the kitchen, where the dog cannot see you, and ask him to tell us how much is two plus two."

Madame Moekel went and stood on the other side of the kitchen door. She commanded Rolf to stay, then closed the door. Several seconds later, her muffled voice could be heard asking, "Rolf, how much are two and two?"

The dog sniffed as he walked past the professors on his way to the table. Up went his paws, and the three men gaped at each other as he tapped the wood two times, barked in a friendly way, and tapped two more times. Then he dropped back to the floor.

The professors had Madame Moekel ask Rolf to solve simple subtraction problems. Rolf did this almost as well as the addition. He had two wrong answers out of ten. At last, the professors were agreed: this was not a trick. The dog *could* add and subtract.

Now that Rolf was famous as the Counting Dog

of Mannheim, Madame Moekel wanted to add to his fame. She tried — and succeeded — in teaching him to read the alphabet. Since the dog could not talk or write, she used arithmetic as his language.

First, she would write a letter on a blackboard. Then she would tell Rolf a number to go with it. For example, the letter "A" was number one, the letter "B" was number two, and so on. To "write" the letter "A," Rolf tapped his paw once; "B" was two taps; "C" was three taps. . . .

But it would have taken too many taps for most of the letters, especially "X" and "Y" and "Z." So Madame Moekel made up a system with short stops between taps. Rolf learned this, too. Instead of tapping on the table, however, he tapped his paw on his mistress's arm.

A very well-known writer of that time, Maurice Maeterlinck, came to see the wonder dog do his arithmetic and talking. Maeterlinck was sure this would turn out to be some sort of clever trickery. But he changed his mind after a Professor Mackenzie had asked Rolf a series of questions and was answered in spelled-out sentences. One such question-and-answer went:

Q. Rolf, what is autumn?

A. Time for apples.

Rolf continued to amuse and amaze people for

five more years. When he died in 1919, the title of wonder dog was passed on to his daughter, Lola. She also could count and read by tapping her paws. And Lola's daughter, owned by a Professor Zielger of Stuttgart, carried on the family tradition. Named Awa, Rolf's granddaughter did arithmetic and drew colored pictures. (There is no explanation of how she did this. Most likely she dipped a paw or her nose in paint, using the paw or nose as a brush.)

One German art critic was asked to watch Awa do a picture. After it was finished, he is supposed to have said, "It is just so-so. Send for me when she has improved her skills."

More seriously, many animal experts tried to explain how Rolf, Lola, and Awa were able to do such miraculous things. None could come up with reasons that made sense. The last words on the subject were, "They did it. How or why? Who knows?"